Collins
SCRABBLE™
BRAND CROSSWORD GAME

junior

Spelling
Activity book

Age 6-7

Published by Collins
An imprint of HarperCollinsPublishers
Westerhill Road
Bishopbriggs
Glasgow G64 2QT
www.harpercollins.co.uk

HarperCollinsPublishers
Macken House, 39/40 Mayor Street Upper, Dublin 1,
D01 C9W8, Ireland

© 2023 Mattel. SCRABBLE™ and SCRABBLE tiles, including S1 tiles, are trademarks of Mattel.

Collins ® is a registered trademark of HarperCollins Publishers Limited

www.collins.co.uk

First published in 2023

© HarperCollins Publishers 2023

ISBN 978-0-00-859116-8

10 9 8 7 6 5 4 3 2 1

All rights reserved. No part of this publication may be reproduced, stored in a retrieval system, or transmitted, in any form or by any means, electronic, mechanical, photocopying, recording or otherwise without the prior permission in writing of the publisher and copyright owners.

The contents of this publication are believed correct at the time of printing. Nevertheless the publisher can accept no responsibility for errors or omissions, changes in the detail given or for any expense or loss thereby caused.

HarperCollins does not warrant that any website mentioned in this title will be provided uninterrupted, that any website will be error free, that defects will be corrected, or that the website or the server that makes it available are free of viruses or bugs. For full terms and conditions please refer to the site terms provided on the website.

A catalogue record for this book is available from the British Library

Printed in India by Multivista Global Pvt. Ltd

If you would like to comment on any aspect of this book, please contact us at the above address or online.

E-mail: dictionaries@harpercollins.co.uk

facebook.com/collinsdictionary
@collinsdict

ACKNOWLEDGEMENTS
All images © Shutterstock.com

CONSONANTS AND VOWELS

The letters in pink boxes in the alphabet below are called consonants.

In Scrabble Junior, some tiles are underlined so they are placed the correct way up during a game.

a	b	c	d	e	f	g	h	i	j	k	l	m
n	o	p	q	r	s	t	u	v	w	x	y	z

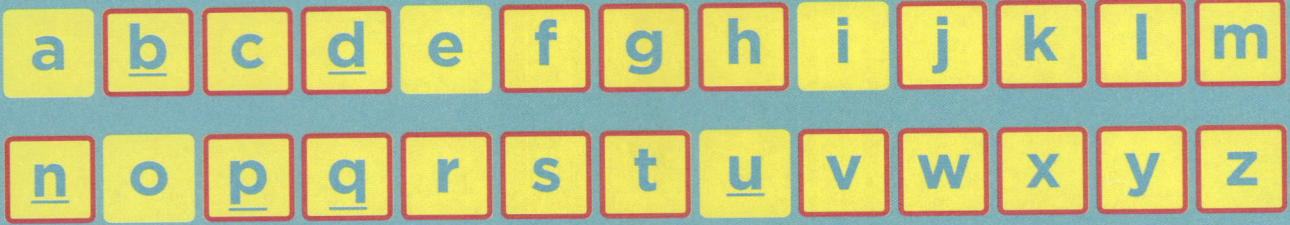

Can you add the missing consonants to the words below?

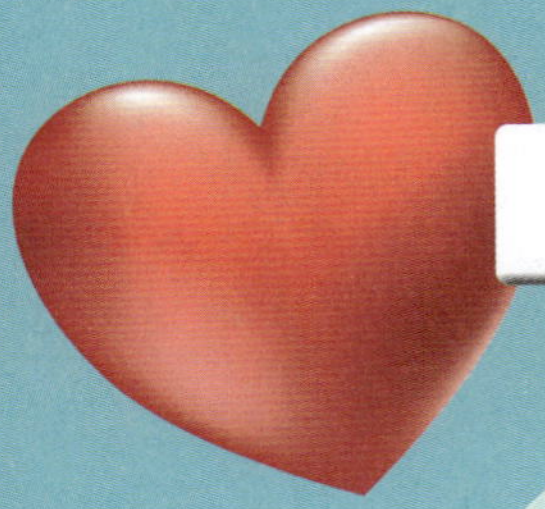

☐ e a r ☐

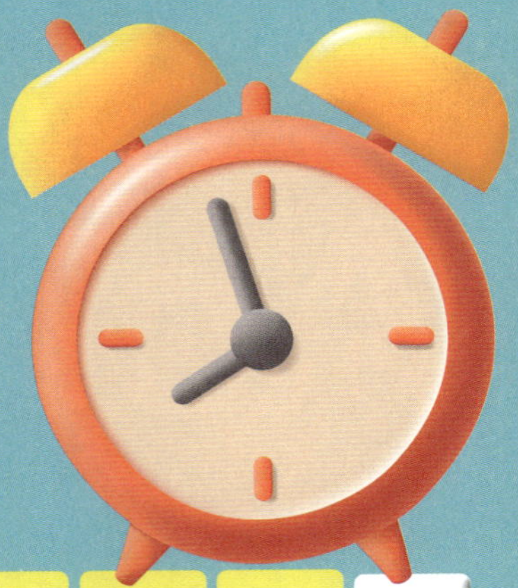

☐ c a r ☐

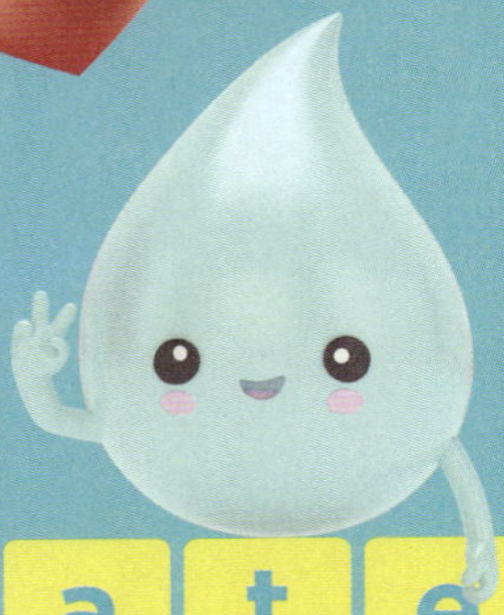

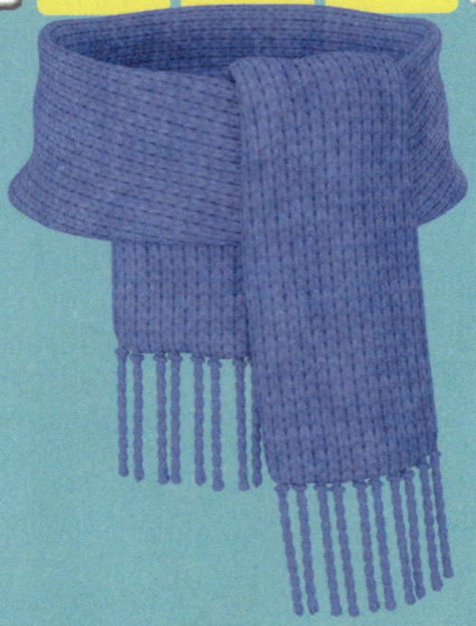

☐ l o c ☐

☐ a t e ☐

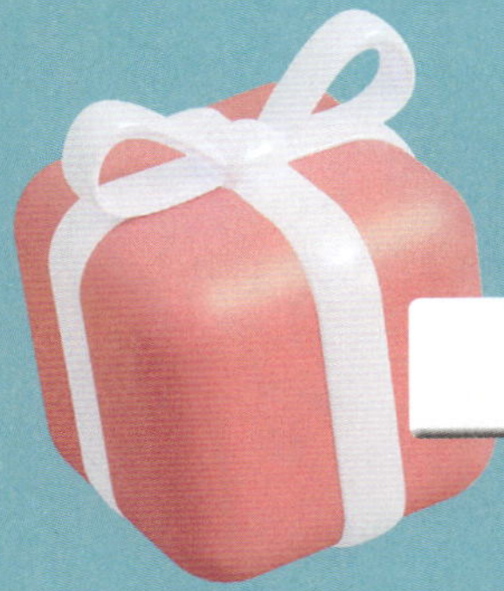

☐ r e s e n ☐

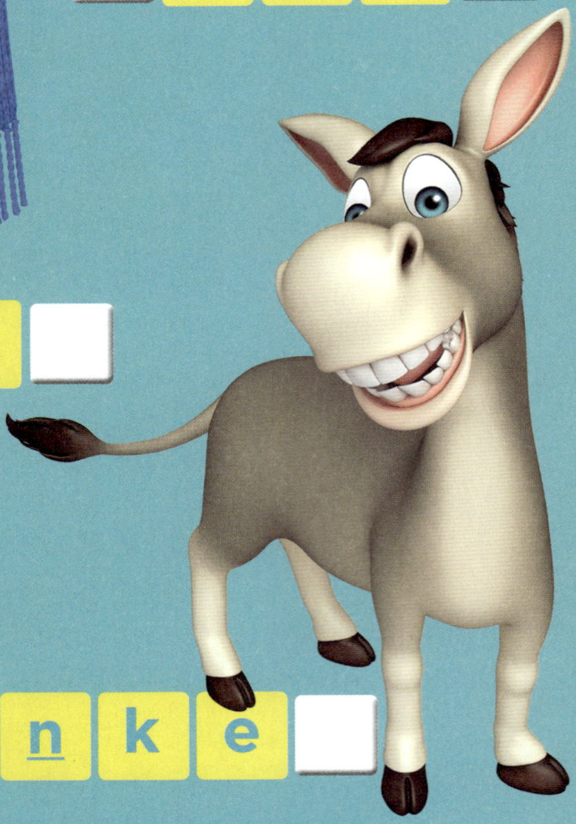

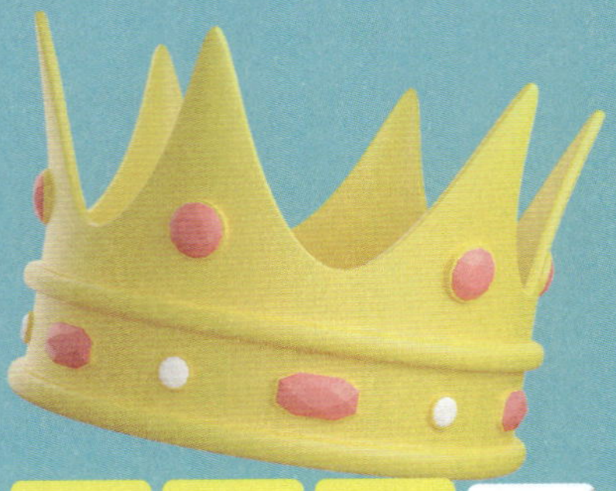

☐ o n k e ☐

☐ r o w ☐

The letters NOT in pink boxes in the alphabet on page 2 are called vowels.

a e i o u

Can you add the missing vowels to the words below?

m _ n k _ y

b _ b i _ s

s q _ _ r _

c _ m p _ t _ r

t r _ _ n g l _

c _ n d l _

r _ b b _ t

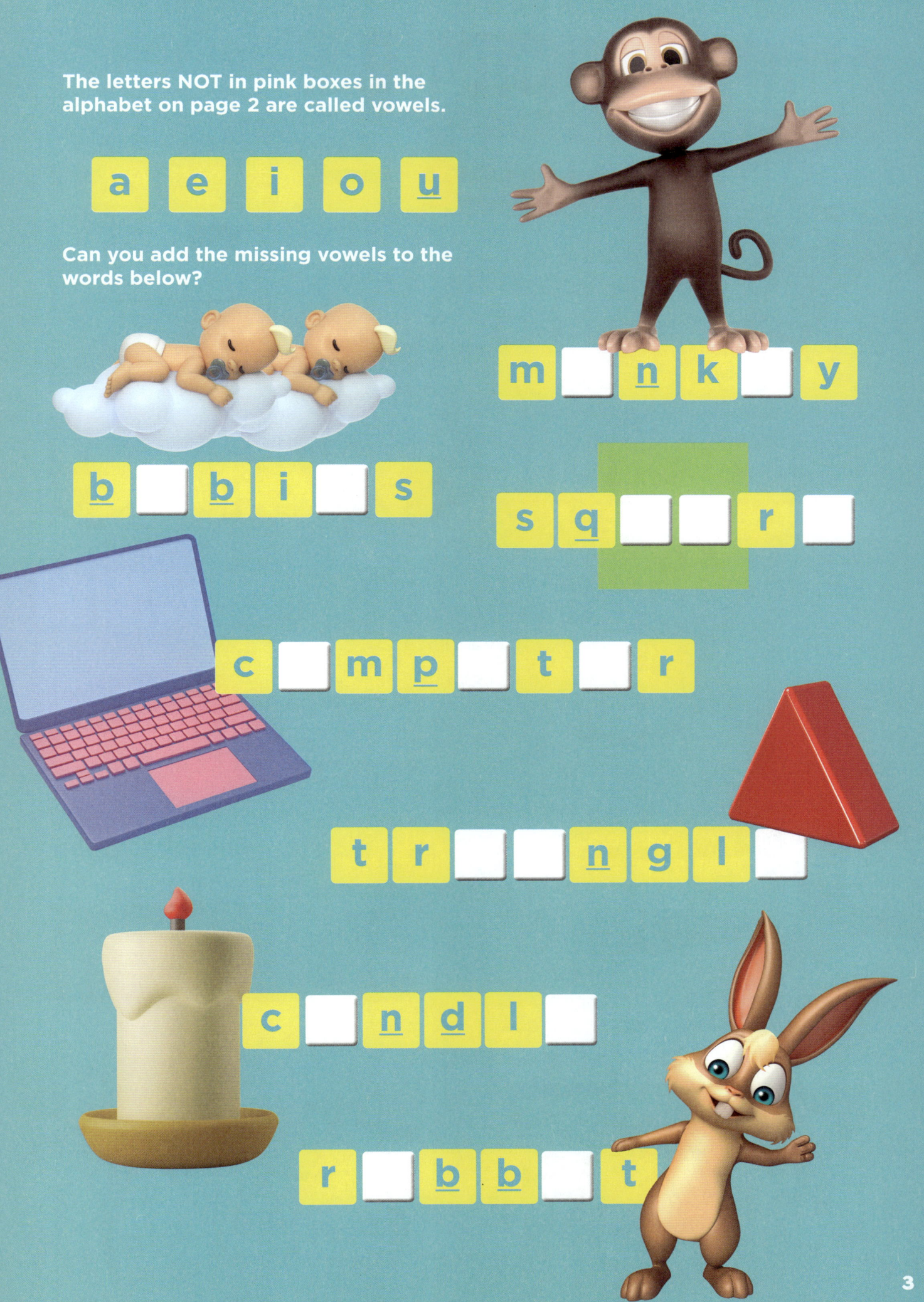

WORDS ENDING -GE OR -DGE

Can you use the clues to find words which end with the letters 'ge' and 'dge'? You might want to use your dictionary to help you.

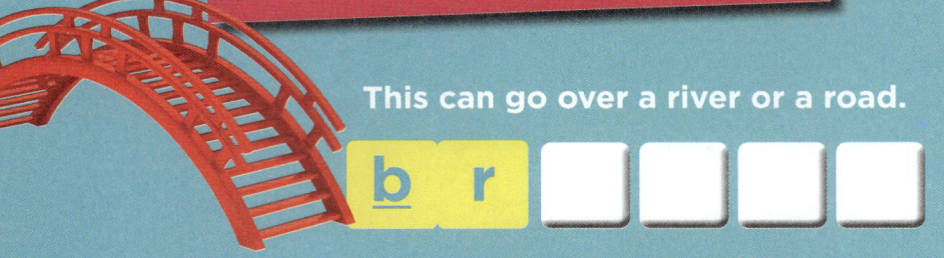

This can go over a river or a road.
b r _ _ _ _

A green vegetable.
c a _ _ _ _ _

A place to keep things cold.
f r _ _ _ _

A very sweet sweet!
f u _ _ _ _

Very big.
h _ _ _

This can separate gardens and fields.
h e _ _ _

Smaller than a town.
v i _ _ _ _ _

Sometimes, the 'r' sound is spelt 'wr' at the beginning of words. This time, 'w' is silent.

Unscramble these words to fill in the crossword with words that start with 'wr'.

- p r w a
- i s t r w
- n g w r i
- e t o r w
- r o n w g
- t r t i e w n
- l e r g g w i
- c k w e r

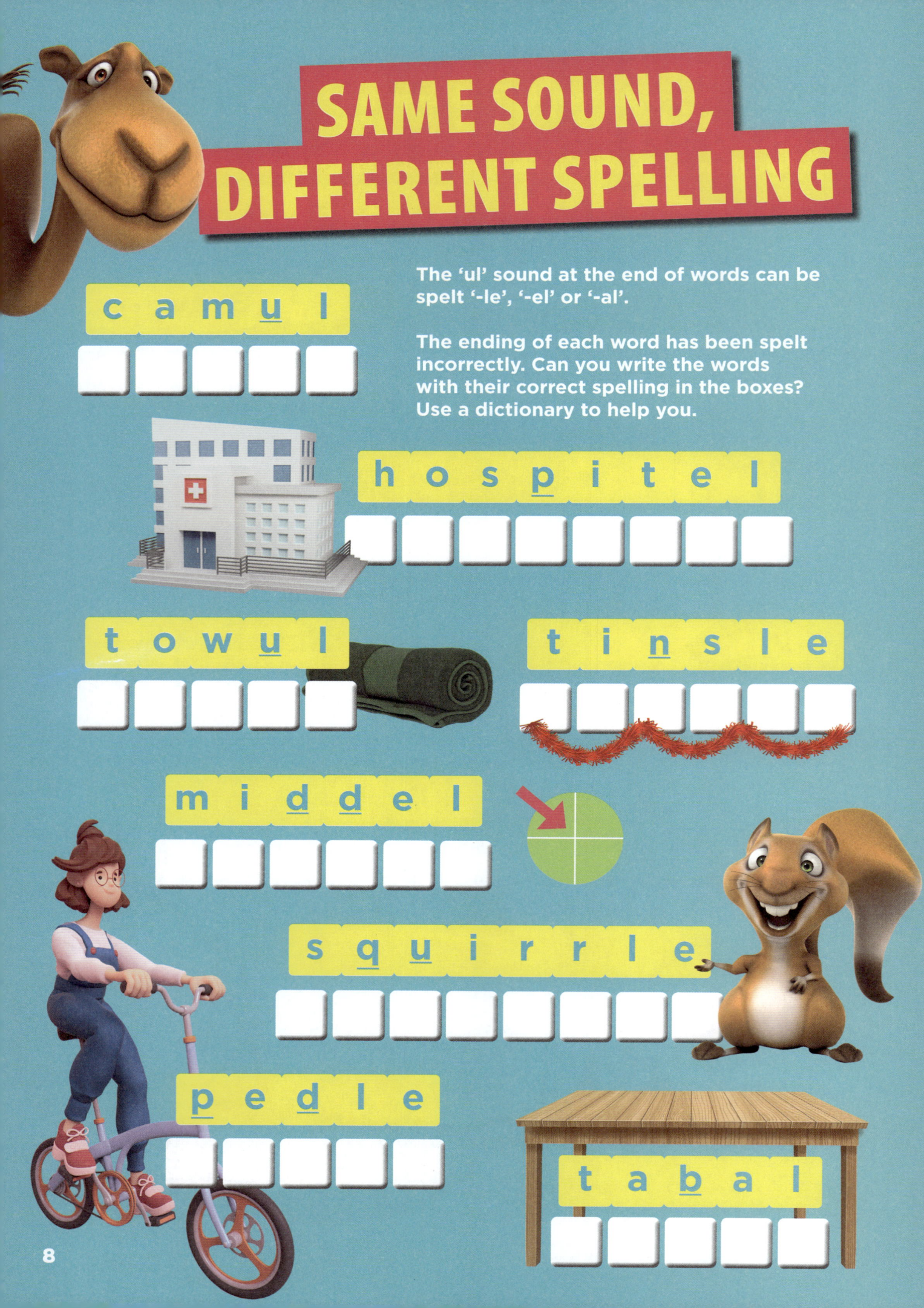

FINDING WORDS

Can you find the words on page 8 in the wordsearch below? There are two extra words for you to find; use the picture clues to help you find these.

```
r w j w f v t t f f t q
r k b b p g h a p w h y
f f e n y r r b y s r e
g b o t t l e l e q c s
t o w e l w w e i u w l
g y g t i n s e l i t a
h o s p i t a l m r r j
q b x l l x d n i r p e
g x a r g u e g d e e g
v e t u n n e l d l d v
s w i e b x t u l x a i
u w i e b c a m e l t
```

WORDS, WORDS AND MORE WORDS!

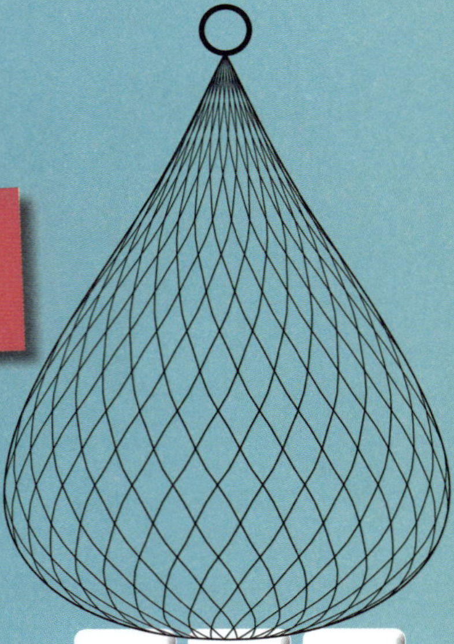

Can you make six 3-letter words using these 5 letters?

e t n p i

Here are 5 different letters. Can you make six more 3-letter words?

r t a o c

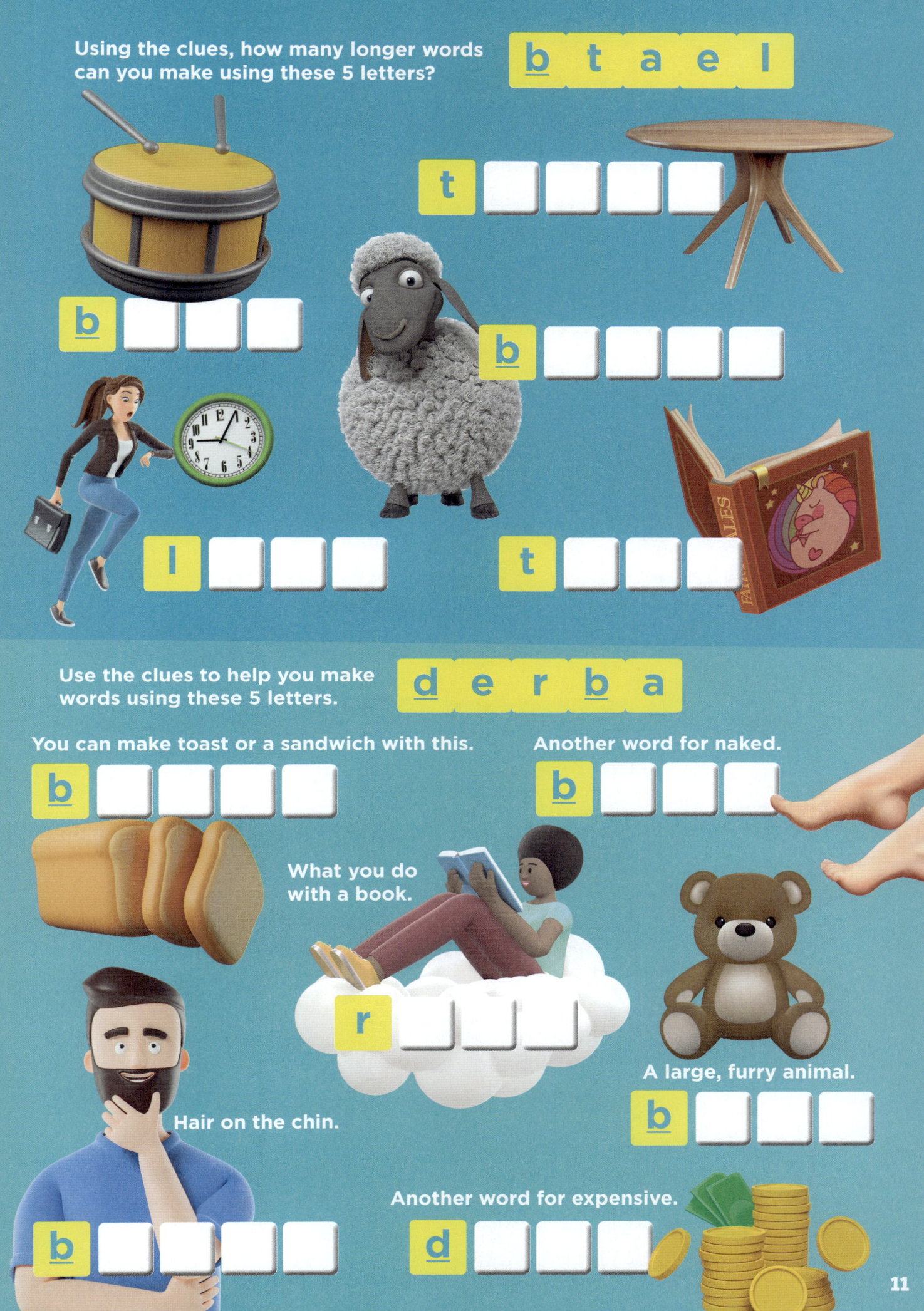

WORDS IN WORDS

The words below have 3-letter words hidden inside them. The letters are in the correct order. For example:

s l i d e

Find the 3-letter words hidden in the words below, then write them in the boxes to the right. Watch out – there might be more than one possible answer so use the picture clues to help you!

f l i p p e r

s p i n e

p a r t y

o r a n g e

s i n k

p r e t e n d

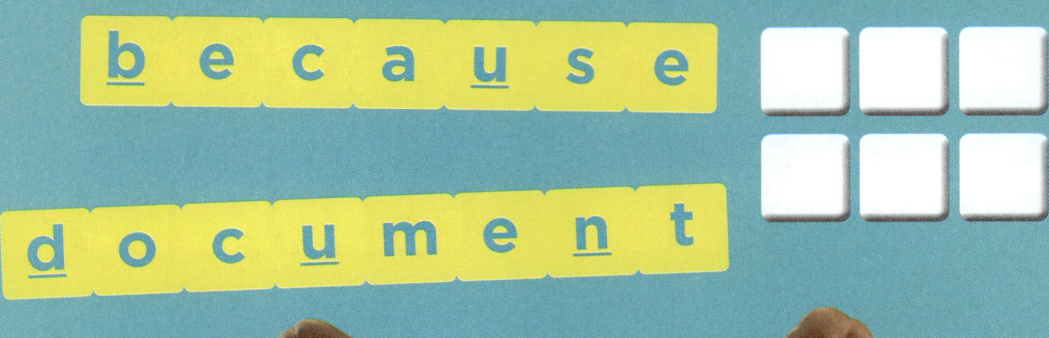

MAKING PLURALS

To make the plural of some words ending in 'y', change the 'y' to 'i' before adding 'es'. For example:

baby → babies

Can you write the plural of these words ending in 'y'?

f a i r y

d r y

c a r r y

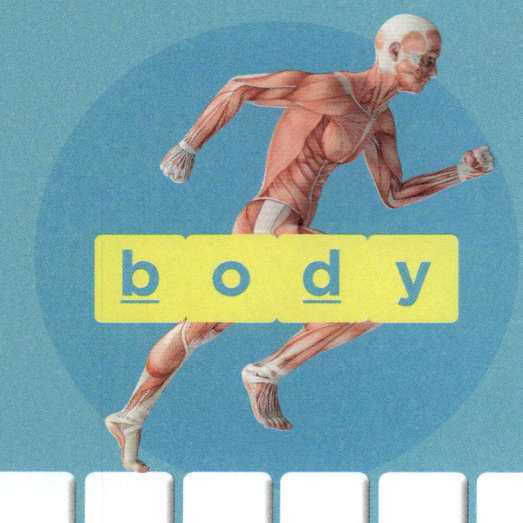

b o d y

s p y

t i d y

WORDSEARCH

Can you find these words that end in 'ies' in the wordsearch below?

- butterflies
- stories
- mysteries
- countries
- families
- replies
- cries
- copies

b	u	t	t	e	r	f	l	i	e	s	g
f	b	a	j	g	s	t	o	r	i	e	s
r	a	q	m	y	s	t	e	r	i	e	s
e	e	m	e	i	p	d	n	z	m	b	e
x	p	p	i	w	w	v	e	c	w	e	v
w	i	e	l	l	t	u	b	o	t	a	w
c	l	c	e	i	i	g	e	p	r	u	g
r	y	r	s	c	e	e	s	i	u	t	k
x	a	i	g	u	e	s	s	e	e	i	t
e	g	e	x	f	w	v	e	s	w	e	l
w	i	s	b	x	t	h	b	x	t	s	u
l	d	c	o	u	n	t	r	i	e	s	z

CHANGING 'Y' TO 'I'

When you add the endings 'ed', 'er' and 'est' to a word ending in 'y' with a consonant before it, you change the 'y' to 'i'. For example:

copy → copied   happy → happier, happiest

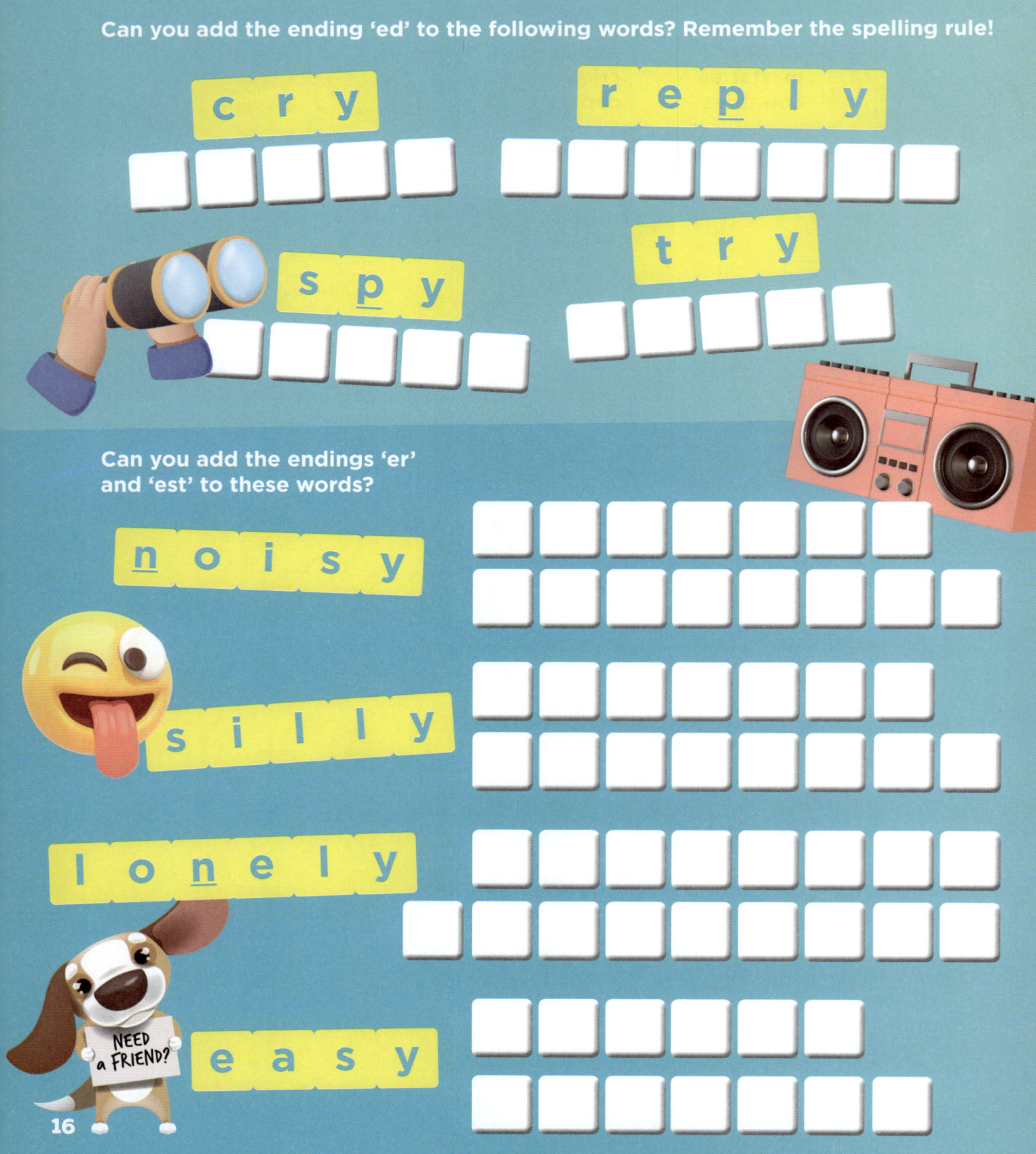

Can you add the ending 'ed' to the following words? Remember the spelling rule!

cry

reply

spy

try

Can you add the endings 'er' and 'est' to these words?

noisy

silly

lonely

easy

CROSSWORD

Finish this crossword using the words you have made on page 16.

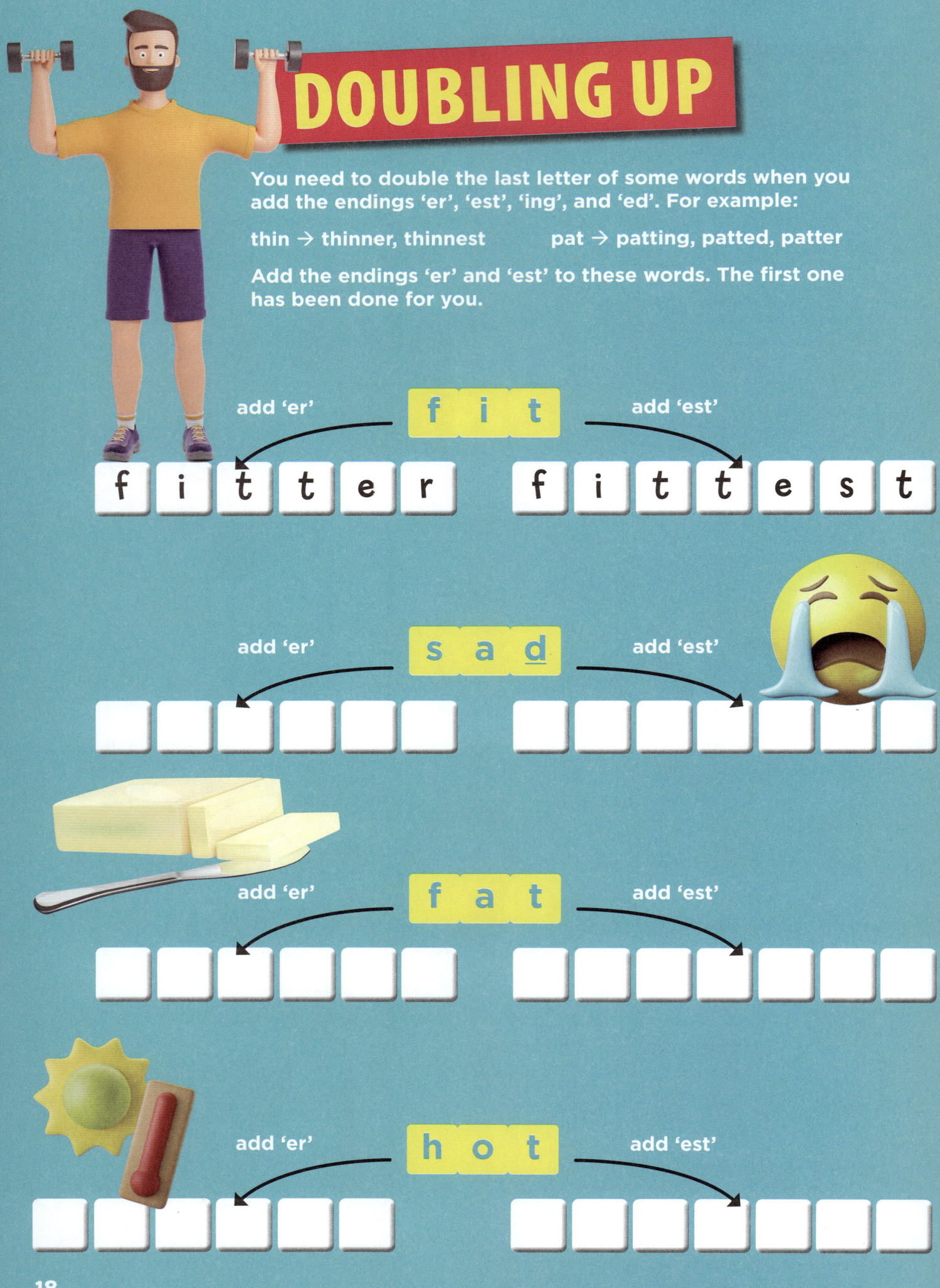

DOUBLING UP

You need to double the last letter of some words when you add the endings 'er', 'est', 'ing', and 'ed'. For example:

thin → thinner, thinnest   pat → patting, patted, patter

Add the endings 'er' and 'est' to these words. The first one has been done for you.

add 'er' ← **f i t** → add 'est'

f i t t e r   **f i t t e s t**

add 'er' ← **s a d** → add 'est'

add 'er' ← **f a t** → add 'est'

add 'er' ← **h o t** → add 'est'

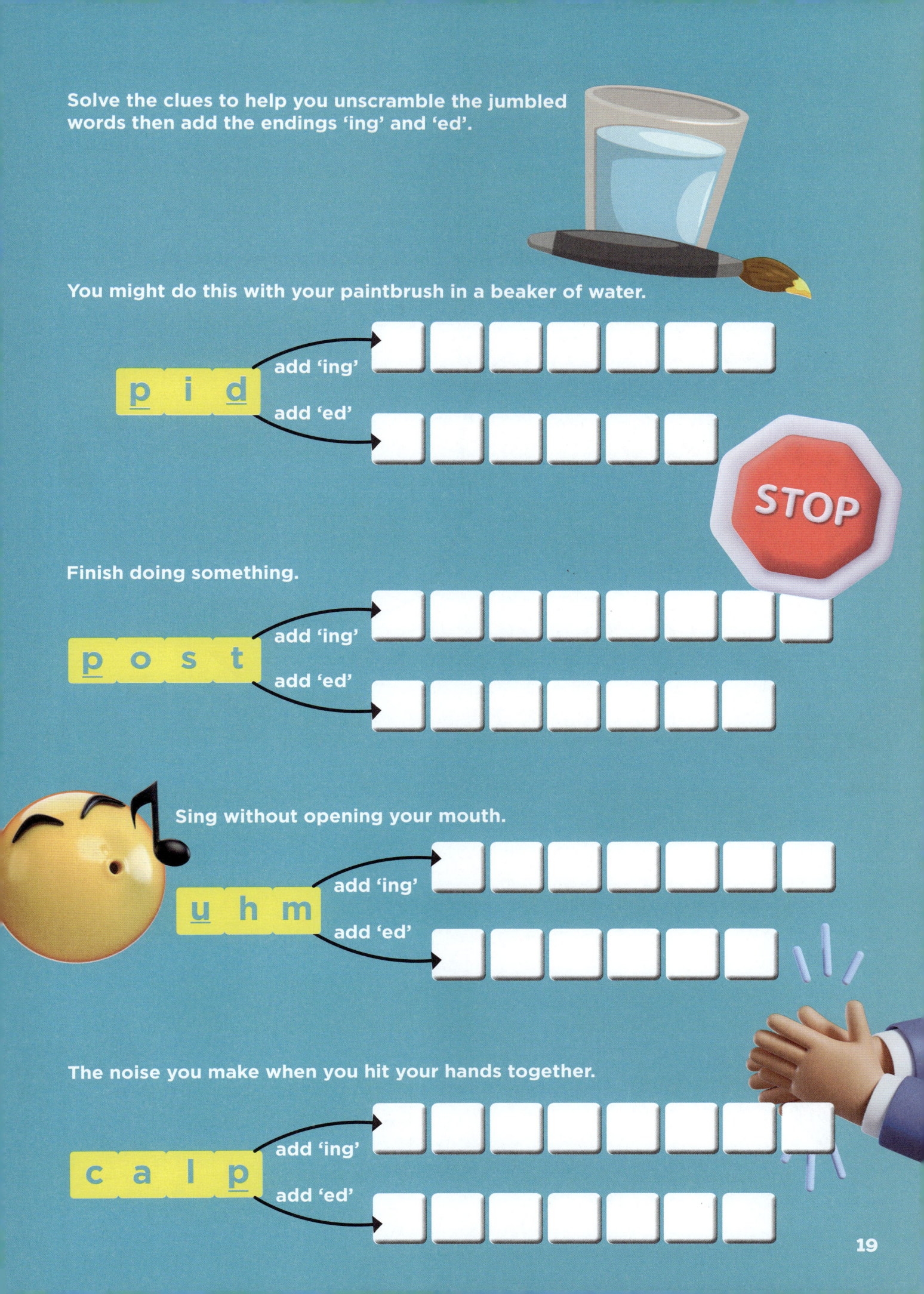

Solve the clues to help you unscramble the jumbled words then add the endings 'ing' and 'ed'.

You might do this with your paintbrush in a beaker of water.

p i d — add 'ing'
add 'ed'

Finish doing something.

p o s t — add 'ing'
add 'ed'

Sing without opening your mouth.

u h m — add 'ing'
add 'ed'

The noise you make when you hit your hands together.

c a l p — add 'ing'
add 'ed'

WORD SUMS

Some words can be joined together to make a new word. For example:

b e d + r o o m = b e d r o o m

Draw a line from a word on the left that can be added to a word on the right to make a new word. One has been done for you.

r a i n → b o w

b i r t h

s h o r t

s n o w

b u t t e r

n e w s

l i g h t

p l a y

c a r

p a i n t

m a n

f l y

b r u s h

b o w

b u l b

d a y

c u t

g r o u n d

p a p e r

p a r k

Now write the word sums from page 20 in the grid below.
The letters in the pink boxes make another word sum.

b
r
p
l
n
c
p
s
s
b

Unscramble each set of letters to make a word, then join them together to make a new word. Some have pictures clues to help you.

eat + top = ☐☐☐☐☐☐

pcu + oabrd = ☐☐☐☐☐☐☐

nair + toac = ☐☐☐☐☐☐☐

hotto + stape =
☐☐☐☐☐☐☐☐☐

LINKING WORDS

Unscramble the letters in each circle to make a word. Write the letters downwards on the grids. Make sure the words across also make sense!

Can you make another word from the letters in pink boxes?

ord

orm

orld

ork

SAME SOUND, DIFFERENT SPELLING

Some words sound the same but are spelt differently. The pairs of words below have been written back-to-front. Can you write each one correctly? The first one has been done for you.

raeh → **hear**   **ereh** → **here**

erab → ____   **raeb** → ____

ees → ____   **aes** → ____

now → ____   **eno** → ____

2 Can you write two more words that sound like the word TWO?

two   ____   ____

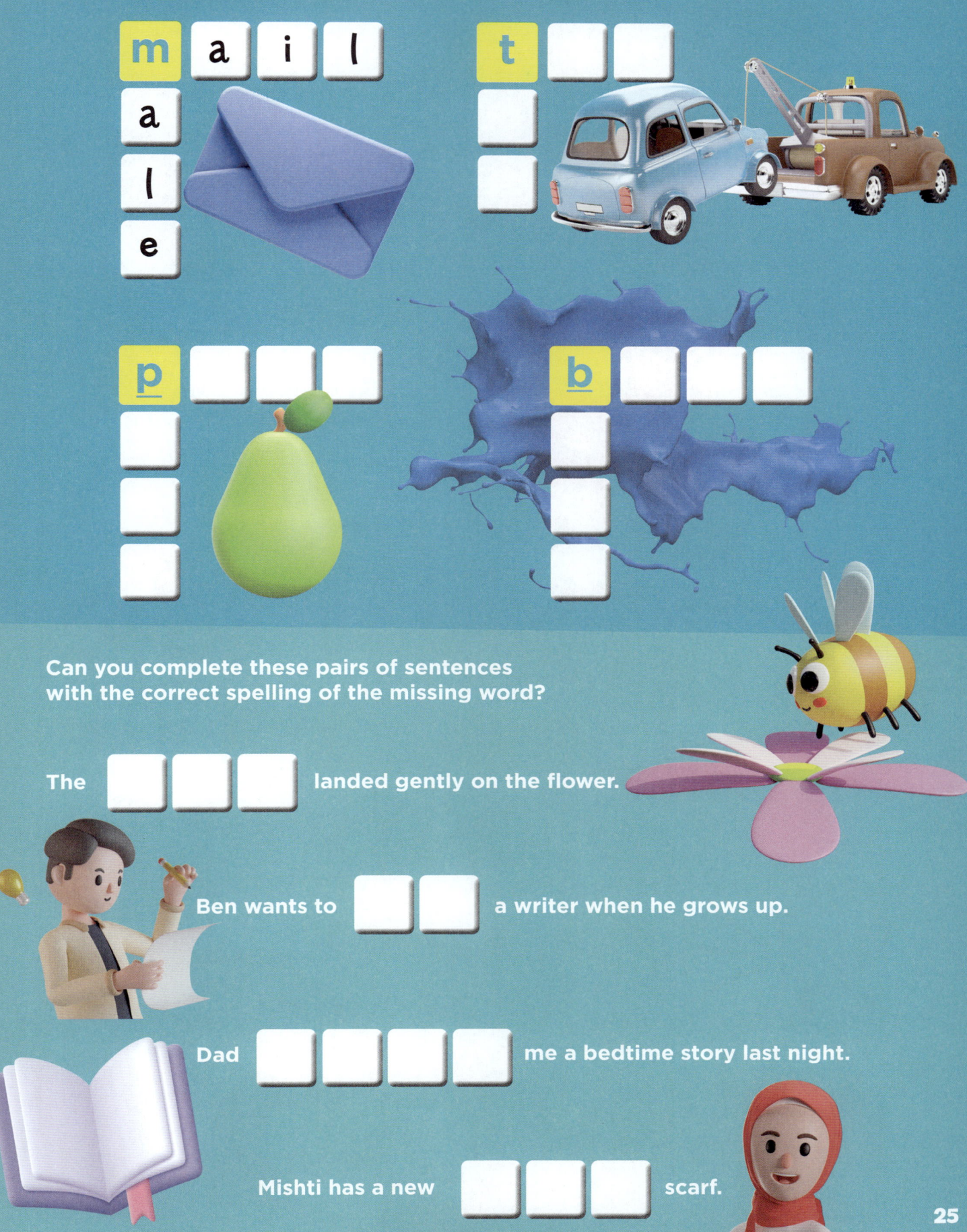

MISSING DOUBLES

These words are missing their middle double letters. Can you fill them in?

ju_ _le

pe_ _er

pa_ _ot

ri_ _on

pi_ _a

sn_ _ze

ke_ _el

WORDS ENDING IN -TION

Can you find these 10 words ending in 'tion' in the wordsearch below?

- section
- motion
- caution
- action
- education
- fiction
- nation
- mention
- station
- ration

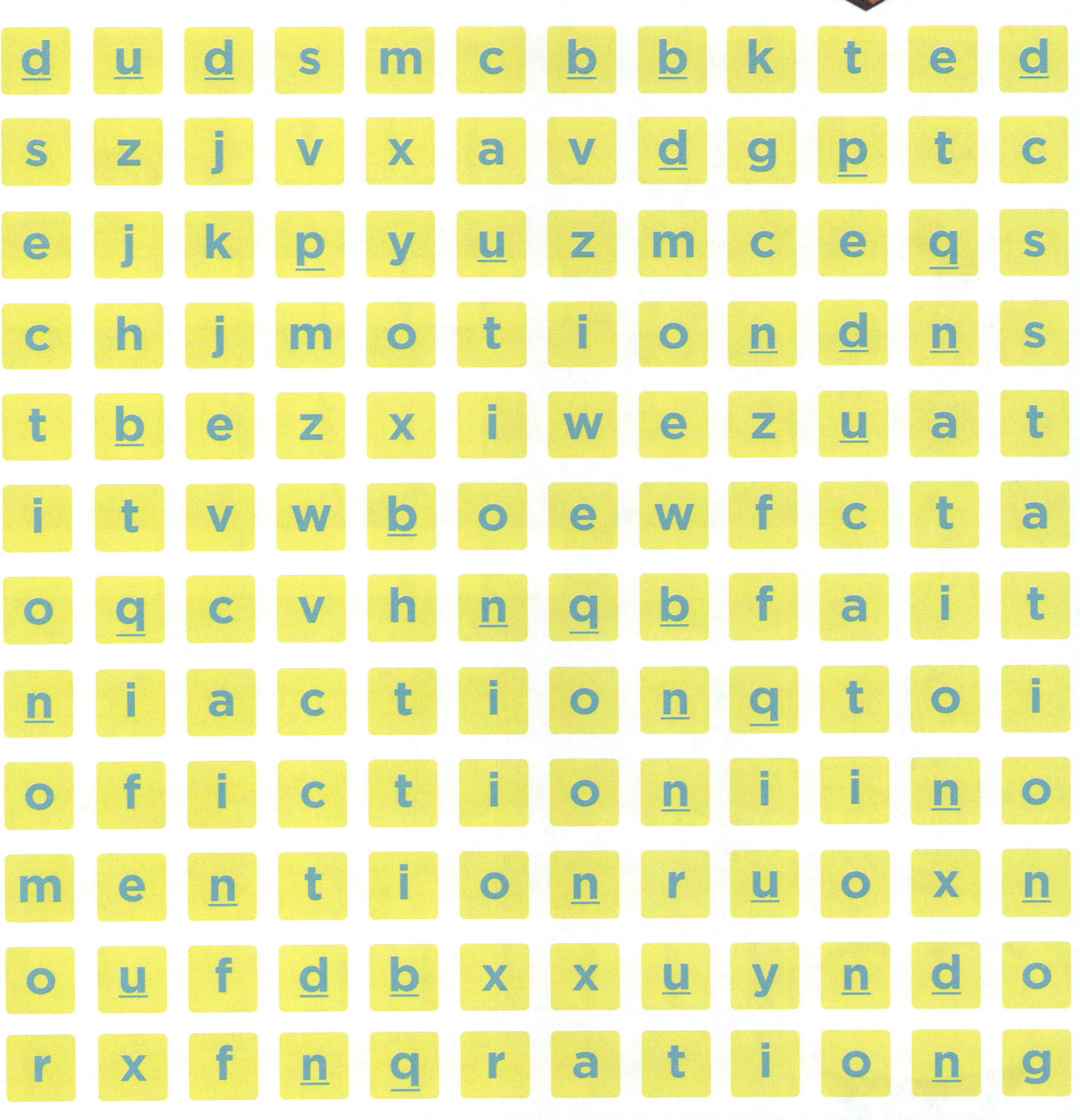

27

ADDING ENDINGS

Can you add the ending 'ment', 'ful', 'less', 'ness' or 'ly' to each of the following words? One has been done for you.

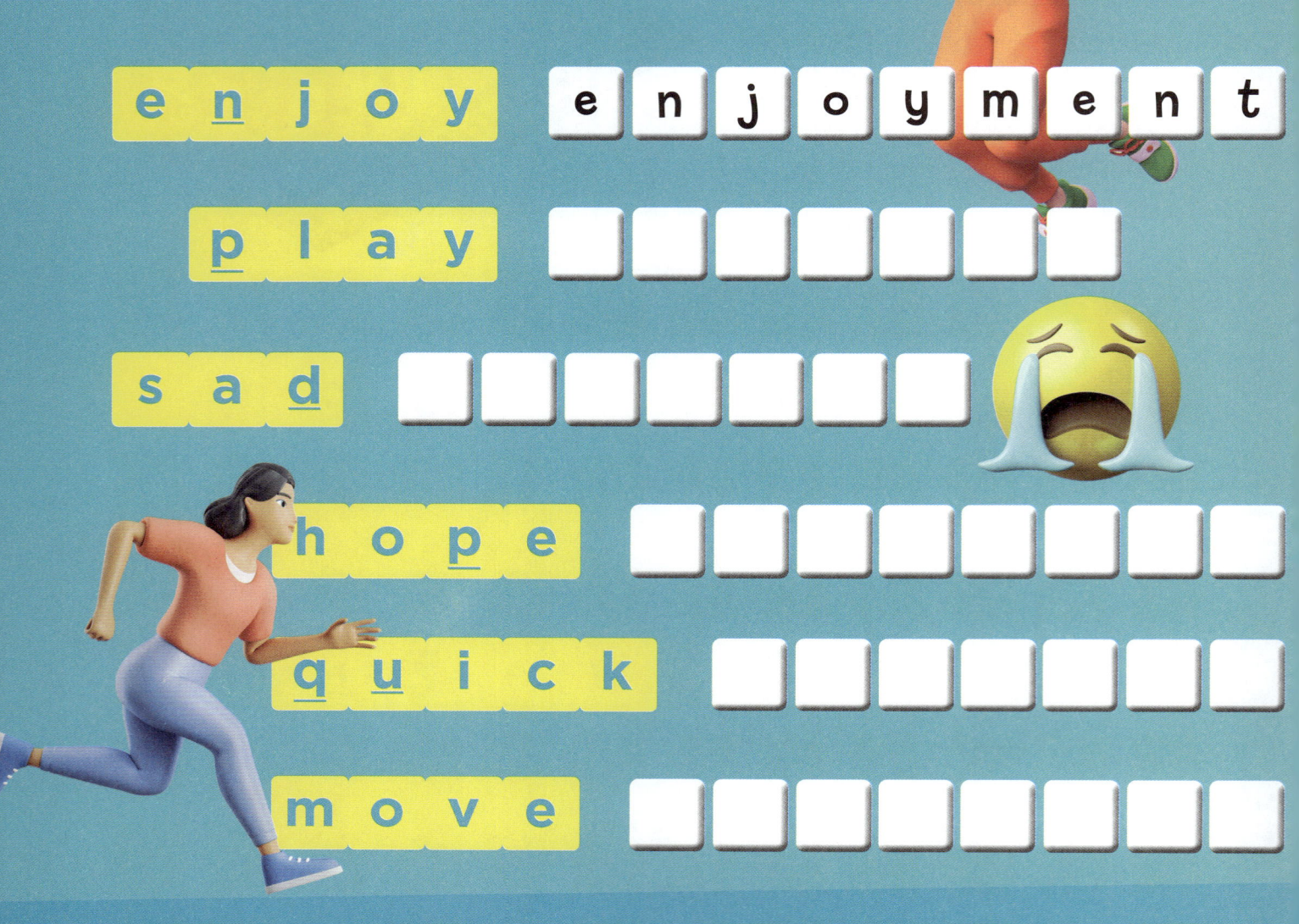

enjoy → enjoyment

play → ☐☐☐☐☐☐☐

sad → ☐☐☐☐☐☐☐

hope → ☐☐☐☐☐☐☐

quick → ☐☐☐☐☐☐

move → ☐☐☐☐☐☐☐

For some words ending in 'y', the 'y' changes to 'i' before the ending is added. For example:

merry → merriment

Can you add the endings 'ness' and 'ly' to the word HAPPY?

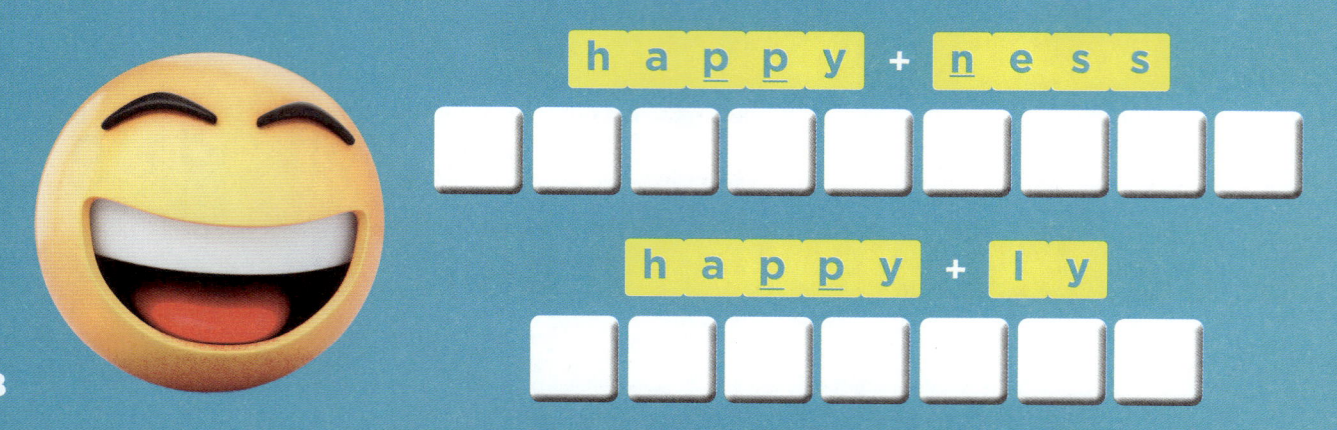

happy + ness
☐☐☐☐☐☐☐☐☐

happy + ly
☐☐☐☐☐☐☐

HIDDEN WORDS

Can you make a 4-letter word using the end of one word and the start of another? Look at the one that has been done for you.

past open
stop

cope stool
☐☐☐☐

cart early
☐☐☐☐

table apple
☐☐☐☐

vest rotten
☐☐☐☐

CROSSWORD CAPERS

Use the clues to finish the crossword.

ACROSS

1. The sound a snake makes.
3. You can find these in rivers or the sea.
5. An animal that makes an OINK sound.
7. How you feel when you are filled with joy.
9. When you speak these move.
10. A strong feeling with your heart.
11. You need one to post a letter or card.

DOWN

2. Opposite of blunt.
4. Sails on the sea.
6. They keep your hands warm.
8. A baby dog.
9. A light you might have on a table.

WORDSEARCH

Find all the 24 words in this house! Cross them off in the cloud below as you find them.

bath	garage	sink
bedroom	iron	stairs
carpet	kettle	table
chair	kitchen	teapot
cushion	lamp	television
door	oven	toaster
freezer	radio	wardrobe
fridge	rug	window

```
            t x
          z e w o
        s t a i r s
      w t p p n r h i         c
    c a e s o d a e r r x a
    a u r l b t o d l o u m r
    t s d e s c w i f n g r p
    t h r v i d e o t a b l e
    i i o i n g a r a g e t t
    c o b s k t x s z f d o f
b c   c n e i f r e e z e r a r
a b h l l r d o o r i t h g o s i
m a a a o v e n k e t t l e o t d
n t i m c g h h e a t e r c m e g
o h r p k i t c h e n e d e f r e
```

ANSWERS

Page 2
heart, scarf, water, clock, present, crown, donkey

Page 3
monkey, babies, square, computer, triangle, candle, rabbit

Page 4
bridge, cabbage, fridge, fudge, huge, hedge, village

Page 5
giraffe, gem, jog, magic, jar, jump, juice

Page 6

Page 7

Pages 8
camel, hospital, towel, tinsel, middle, squirrel, pedal, table

Page 9

Page 10
tie, pen, net, pie, pin, ten
arc, cot, cat, car, oar, rat

Page 11
table, beat, bleat, late, tale
bread, bare, read, bear, beard, dear

Page 12
lip, pin, art, ran, ink, ten

Page 13
tea, ice, bow, par, tow, rot, use, men

Page 14
fairies, dries, carries, bodies, spies, tidies

Page 15

Page 16
cried, replied, spied, tried

noisier, noisiest   sillier, silliest
lonelier, loneliest   easier, easiest

Page 17

Page 18
sadder, saddest   fatter, fattest
hotter, hottest

Page 19
dipping, dipped   stopping, stopped
humming, hummed   clapping, clapped

Page 20
birthday, shortcut, snowman, butterfly, newspaper, lightbulb, playground, carpark, paintbrush

Page 21
butterfly, rainbow, paintbrush, lightbulb, newspaper, carpark, playground, snowman, shortcut, birthday
tablecloth

teapot, cupboard, raincoat, toothpaste

Page 22
flew, claw, jaw, slow

crowd

Page 23

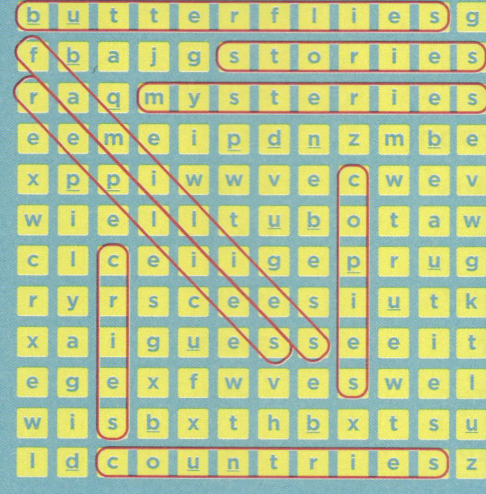

Page 24
bare, bear   see, sea   won, one
to, too

Page 25
toe, tow   pear, pair   blue, blew
bee, be   read, red

Page 26
juggle, pepper, parrot, ribbon, pizza, sneeze, kennel

Page 27

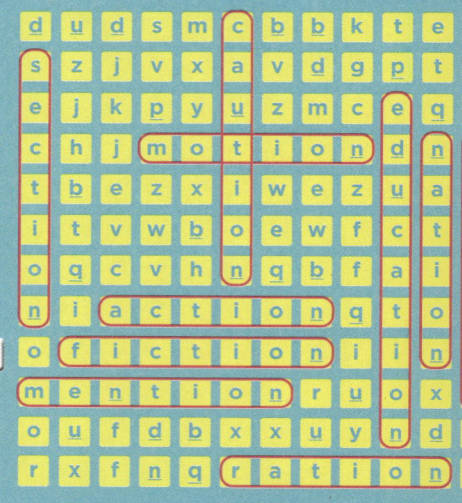

Page 28
playful, sadness, hopeless, quickly, movement
happiness, happily

Page 29
pest, tear, leap, trot

Page 30
Across
1. hiss 3. fish 5. pig 7. happy 9. lips
10. love 11. stamp
Down
2. sharp 4. ship 6. gloves 8. puppy
9. lamp

Page 31